Cyclone Scare

By Ken Bonson

Illustrated by Jasurbek Ruzmat

Library For All Ltd.

Library For All is an Australian not for profit organisation with a mission to make knowledge accessible to all via an innovative digital library solution. Visit us at libraryforall.org

Cyclone Scare

First published 2024

Published by Library For All Ltd
Email: info@libraryforall.org
URL: libraryforall.org

Our Yarning logo design by Jason Lee, Bidjipidji Art

Original illustrations by Jasurbek Ruzmat

Cyclone Scare
Bonson, Ken
ISBN: 978-1-923143-49-4
SKU04313

Cyclone Scare

We respect and honour Aboriginal and Torres Strait Islander Elders past, present and future. We acknowledge the stories, traditions and living cultures of Aboriginal and Torres Strait Islander peoples on this land and commit to building a brighter future together.

Poppa Ken was a firefighter in Darwin when he was young.

He had been on duty when Cyclone Tracy hit in 1974 and destroyed the whole town on Christmas Eve.

He said he'd never been so scared in his life, and hoped we would never have to go through something so scary.

It had been raining hard for several days, and the fire crew were getting the engine truck ready to go out and help people.

But then, the police called and ordered the crew not to go out — the cyclone was too strong!

They all tried to stay brave while they waited at the fire station, but they were worrying about their families.

Before long, it was midnight, and it was too dangerous to go out into the street: heavy rain, lightning, deafening thunder, and terrible winds shook the town.

The crew watched debris being blown away along the road as rain sleeted down sideways.

The ceiling of the engine room bounced and shook so hard they thought it would collapse on them.

Poppa Ken and the other firefighters moved into the duty office to wait out the cyclone.

The wind howled.

Then, without warning, the air was completely sucked out of the room. A station wall was blown away into the blackness of the night.

Poppa Ken grabbed the door frame.
His mates all grabbed on to rails and
were being blown horizontally — they
were hanging on for their life!

One crew member close to the wall was slammed into the corner and nearly sucked out into the night. But he held on tight.

When it was safe to do so, everyone moved into a storeroom and waited for hours, listening as the cyclone raged.

Five tornadoes hit Darwin that night. It was the worst in the city's history.

Everyone in the station knew it would soon be time to see the damage and help people.

By six o'clock in the morning, Poppa Ken and his mates saw it had calmed enough to leave.

They tried to drive out to see what damage had been done. But the truck's wheels were punctured twice within minutes of being outside in the storm.

Poppa Ken couldn't wait any more and walked home to find his family.

Poppa Ken began to walk through the rain towards where his house was.

He couldn't tell which direction he was going. And his normal five-minute walk home took him two hours.

Poppa Ken had to struggle through knee-high rushing water, as water had turned the roads into rivers.

Fences, signposts, and roofs were all missing. Houses and walls were destroyed. And debris floated everywhere.

People started coming out of their houses, laughing and crying in shock.

Finally, Poppa Ken found his house and saw the roof had been blown off.

His family had sheltered in a bedroom upstairs, safe under a mattress.

Poppa Ken ran up the back stairs searching for them, and they ran down the front stairs calling his name.

When they finally found each other, they hugged, laughing and crying with relief.

Everyone was safe.

The cyclone terrorised Darwin for more than five hours and destroyed 80 percent of the city.

People around Australia and the world saw what happened and helped Darwin to recover and rebuild.

Santa didn't get to deliver the presents to the children of Darwin that night, but Poppa Ken said the best present of all was that his family was safe.

You can use these questions to talk about this book with your family, friends and teachers.

What did you learn from this book?

Describe this book in one word. Funny? Scary? Colourful? Interesting?

How did this book make you feel when you finished reading it?

What was your favourite part of this book?

About the author

Ken is a Jawoyn and Thursday Island man. He was born and grew up in Darwin, where he spent many years as a firefighter. Now, he lives in Adelaide, close to his daughter and her family. He is a proud grandad and great grandad. He loves reading stories to his grandchildren.

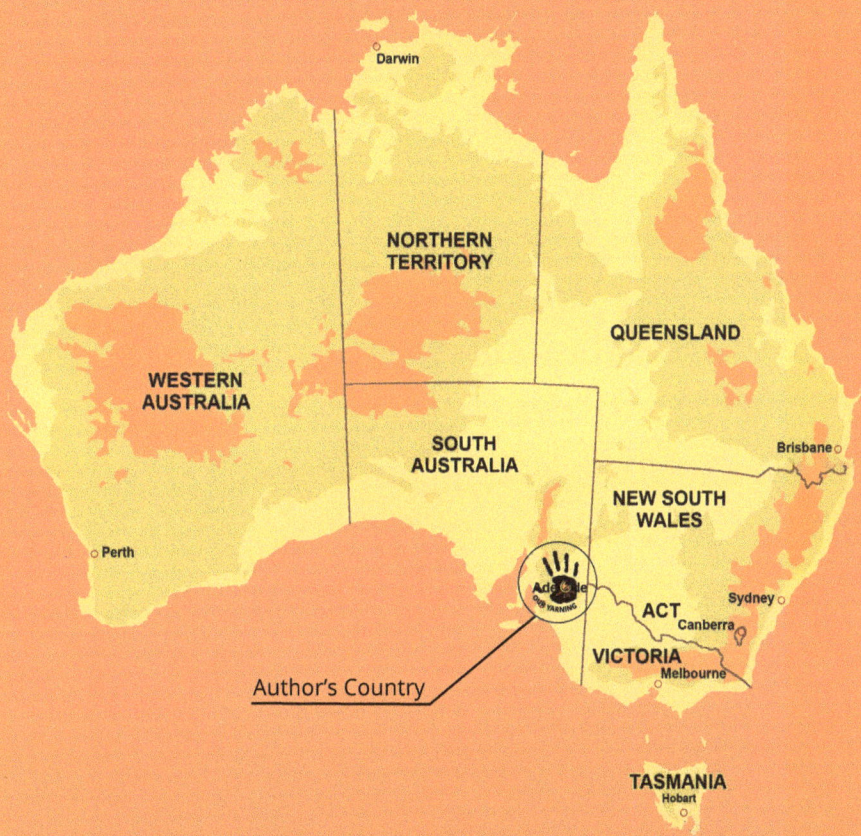

Darwin

NORTHERN
TERRITORY

QUEENSLAND

WESTERN
AUSTRALIA

SOUTH
AUSTRALIA

Brisbane

NEW SOUTH
WALES

Perth

Adelaide

Sydney

ACT

Canberra

VICTORIA

Melbourne

Author's Country

TASMANIA

Hobart

Our Yarning

Want to discover more books from this collection? Our Yarning is a collection of books written by Aboriginal and Torres Strait Islander peoples across Australia.

We know that children learn better, and enjoy reading more, when they see themselves in the stories, characters and illustrations of the books they read.

To download the app, visit the Google Play Store on any Android device and search 'Our Yarning'.

libraryforall.org

www.ingramcontent.com/pod-product-compliance
Lightning Source LLC
Chambersburg PA
CBHW042343040426
42448CB00019B/3392